Also from Telling Our Stories Press

IMPACT: An Anthology of Short Memoirs
ROLL: A Collection of Personal Narratives
SURVIVE: A Collection of Short Memoirs
TURNS: A Collection of Memoir Chapbooks
SO LONG: Short Memoirs of Loss and Remembrance
THE BRIDGE: A Companion Journal for Unearthing Personal Narratives and Memoir
RESURRECTING PROUST: Unearthing Personal Narratives through Journaling

More Praise for McCord:

"The pared inscription, as well as the delicacy and discretion, of Katherine McCord's debut collection, Island, are always deeply compelling and often breathtaking. The honorable simplicity of this work rewards us time and time again with both wisdom and delight. Quietly elegant, and as intimate as a whisper, this is a book to hold close in the silence of night."
~David St. John, author of *The Auroras*

"McCord's is a searching poetry, asking questions that have answers too hard to bear."
—Sheila Cowing, author of *Jackrabbit Highways* and *Stronger in the Broken Places*

"Katherine McCord explodes triumphantly onto the poetry scene with her newest collection of prose poems . . . She writes with fevered delicacy. . .and offers us an astounding package. This is the work of a mature, talented writer who integrates her personal amazement at the details of daily life with the inescapable act of being an artist . . . It is deeply compelling work that speaks to the artist's method and madness with delicious effect . . . McCord gives us a year of her life and it is a privilege to experience it through her passionate language."
—Jeanie C. Williams, co-editor of *Saludos! Poemas*

"Sometimes from dry ground some of the most important and exciting poetry springs. From the saturated reds and greens of New Mexico comes the moving lyric of a life told in poems. Katherine McCord's poems captured me from the first line. . . and carried me through their autobiography in poems. I knew it was a book I had to pay attention to and it's a collection I am proud to have had some small part in bringing to the public. It's the big emptiness of the desert sky crying out to be filled that pulls these lines from the poet's heart. It's a cool cloth on the dying man's brow, the only comfort for miles and the only comfort needed."
—Robert Bixby, author of *Come Along*

"[Katherine McCord] is a remarkable poet whose work is certain and hesitant at once, compressed and expansive. She wants silence to speak as carefully as her words. She sees poetry in the purest sense, working toward pieces where important things aren't merely described or reported but transformed. Katherine McCord is an artist, through and through, taking aspects of ordinary life and finding fear and wonder in them."
—Marianne Boruch, author of *Grace, Fallen from* and *In the Blue Pharmacy*

Katherine McCord's moving sequence of prose poems, Living Room, expresses truthfully and with poignant, even painful clarity the trials and triumphs of a life claimed by conflicting loves: love of writing, love of husband and children. She gives us a year of this life, and it is a privilege to experience it through her evocative, passionate language.
—Kelly Cherry, author of *The Retreats of Thought* and *The Woman Who*

MY CIA

MY CIA

A Memoir

Katherine McCord

Telling Our Stories Press

Showcasing the Art of Literary Personal Narratives

Published by Telling Our Stories Press

The independent literary imprint with a focus on
the art of short memoir and
personal narratives.

Copyright ©2012 by Katherine McCord
All rights reserved

Library of Congress Control Number: 2011933205

No part of this book may be reproduced or transmitted
in any form or by any means, electronic or mechanical, including
photocopying, recording, or by any information storage and retrieval
system without written permission from the author, except for the
inclusion of brief quotations in a review.

Excerpts from Parts I and II appear in South Loop Review, Volume 11,
and are used by permission of the author.

Excerpts from "Blowback" appear in Fogged Clarity, December 2009,
and are used by permission of the author.

Requests for information should be forwarded to
Telling Our Stories Press
visit
www.TellingOurStoriesPress.com

Cover Design by Chris Schramm
Typeset and book layout by Chris Schramm

Printed in the United States of America

ISBN-13: 978-0982922842
ISBN-10: 0982922841

For *Tom,* *Greta* and *Adi*
again and again and again. . . .

and for my mother and my father
and my sister and my brothers
and my brother-in-law and my nieces. . . .

"O, my god," Sylvia said, "O, my god, what am I / That these late mouths should cry open / In a forest of *frost*, in a *dawn* of cornflowers." --my italics.

It seemed there was a room for playing house--

a kitchen, dolls.

And then indecipherable things.

Finally, a heart I made with glue.

The boy across. His head on his folded arms.

Until I can't take it anymore. And everything,

Everything is a dare. Becomes love.

Explodes into words.

Day by day my father flies backwards.

And the pure black dog who was true.

The inside light of winter

and the last few leaves shine through.

Like the book I read with its anguish.

I say, to anyone, it is true.

I tell my students, read it.

It will change you through.

I. Blowback

And where were her people? Spun tight? Deep?

(for Greta and Adi)

"'Blowback' is a CIA term first used in March 1954…It is a metaphor for the unintended consequences of the US government's international activities that have been kept secret from the American people."

—Chalmers Johnson

I write a book for her. Then my sister and I dredge up the past. And after the last kid is sealed inside, we ride to the sound of phones. The house and life before me. The fan fires. The light flickers. An explosion behind the jets in the sky. We call it Sun. From a friend's we go on a walk. See a house behind hollyhocks swaying in lanes. Fixated, I'm uprooted by my sister's hand. Come on, she says. I don't remember ever being so far from home. At the hospital stairs are carpeted like tires. A Coke machine dispenses cups for a quarter. It is our childhood. We race. Choose the best-damned one.

So I list things. Like where I can no longer go. A series of sagging second-story porches. And how upon waking I see it. That the mirror reflects the truth. Like a bullet hole.

So oblivion's a mirror. Shame intermingles. How to proceed with the body and heart and soul you've been given. Then there are two trees. Red apples. White. Prodigious. Scarce. Separated by a path. The thunk of a prize tumbling down a shaft slow.

And what's *with* the shoes? Always upright. Unlaced. One of two. At the same intersection. All winter. Dispersed. As if some of us are lifted, willing ourselves to stay intact.

II. My CIA

What I have to tell you is that I don't know why my father, the CIA, my three trips to a healer, and the Sisters of Bon Secours labyrinth are linked. But they all pulse in my mind with the same uncertainty. Like in the story, *A Wrinkle In Time*, that I read as a child. At the climax there's a dais. On the dais is something the main character has to face. It throbs. If I remember right, I think it was the main character herself. Surrounding the dais are members of the main character's family. Unconscious. Dreaming. Held together by strobes. Anyway, what I know now, about each of these things is that 1. I miss my father terribly and what has replaced him is nothing. But longing and a wanting to understand the mystery behind his existence. So, because of the Freedom of Information Act, I wrote to the CIA and asked them for information about my father's work for them. What he did in Africa, Nepal, and Vietnam. Maybe to understand him, but more, I think, to find the connection between his past and my present life. 2. Because of health issues, I sought a physical therapist I thought might be a healer too. She describes herself to me as an energy worker. All I know is that she can read my mind. And when she's working on me, she sees what I see. Without knowing my ability to fly, she says to me when things start to become difficult, *Now, don't start flying.* Just as I'm envisioning myself standing on earth, heels up, milliseconds before pushing off. Arms outspread. 3. I don't know any of the Sisters of Bon Secours. Their website describes the convent's mission as "to help bring people to wholeness, to alleviate human suffering, and to help bring others to a deeper awareness of their own spirituality." And that the labyrinth is "a symbolic pilgrimage or journey to the divine." Coincidentally, my healer's last name is Devine.

My healer says she is peeling back layers. She says my body is in a state of pensiveness. Bated breath. She says she needs to drain the bad blood. Blood, she adds, that isn't mine. And just before she says it, I'm looking down into a tunnel where a dark reddish brown liquid flows.

I look up "bad blood" in the dictionary. It is bitterness between persons. I decide to go to the Sisters of Bon Secours labyrinth. It is just up the road.

On the way home from seeing *Bobby*, a monumental film set in 1968, the headlights of my husband's car catch the sign for the Sisters of Bon Secours convent, reminding me to find out how one can visit.

I want my healer to understand without my having to ask. I want her to tell me exactly what I need to do to get on with my life. I want her to tell me whose bitterness I carry.

I'm hoping the letter about my father will come soon, that everything will make sense. Symbols and times and locations. Like 1968, the year of the setting of *Bobby*. The year I was four. The year my father began his last mission. Each will shine with a resonance beyond my knowing; the knowing will make me whole.

In the meantime, I call the Public Information Line at the CIA asking for a time frame. Sooner than later, I get, even though I first contacted them over a year ago, six months after my father died.

***

My healer says I need to pick *an* issue. That I'm all over the place today. In my body. Out of my body. Downright confused. I tell her I'm not sure where to go. The pain in my abdomen has lessened and all tests have come up clean, but sometimes I can't walk upright it's so bad. I want to crawl in bed and curl over it, on my side. Then sleep. Sleep to dream. My healer says things must be better, I'm wearing color and my face is bright. I think it's hope. Hope, because my healer can read my mind. If that's possible, what else is? I try to settle down and concentrate. We talk chakras and I attempt to follow. It seems there's a path between them. I've got to keep them open. Problems, questions need to be filtered through. Blue, green. And gold is the color of a spirit, a spirit that seems to be helping me out. When I leave I feel like I'm going with the wind. And, boy, is it cold. I tell my spirit to fly behind me, try and keep up, cause I'm late, late, late.

***

It's fun, I tell myself, to look for signs. The sun is a bright knee. There's one, and two is in the mailbox, a sealed plain white envelope, a Bible verse inside with some sort of proclamation about the second coming. The mask of a lunatic. I decide it's from the CIA. My house is a container for such things. Some people decorate. I place small objects, bits of paper, letters on tables in teetering piles. It's a game, my husband says, like Jenga.

***

Today the labyrinth has lost its meaning. I think I'll see a bird swoop low over my path? Hear footsteps? One can only take so much mysticism, poignant moments, dark signs. Being "open" takes a lot of work. For now, I'd like to not worry about it and whip through the aisles of Walmart. Not think about every item produced by a man or woman who has never heard of the likes of fair trade. Psychosis is just a breakdown of resistance anyway, resistance to what we already know, all at the same time. I've met my fair share of lunatics in Walmart. Let's face it, when we're in Walmart, we're all on the edge. My sister and I discuss this topic frequently. My Walmart is 10.3 miles from the labyrinth. I clocked it. Just because I don't go in, doesn't mean I can't drive by.

***

I can't rise up out of the muck, the split sun, the dusty streets, the creases in my hands that dry and crack and split and itch. I can't find my favorite anthology of form poetry. I crawl around in the dust. I audition my life and get booted. Onto the next tryout and show. It's avoidance anyway. I build a wall of dishes and voices. In downstairs rooms. They crash together, crash around. Between errands, I slide my two girls' Christmas pictures into envelopes. Then ratchet down, go into numb and subdued.

***

The insurance company wants me to spar with them over coverage. My physical therapist is treating pain in my abdomen, I say, weakly, a timbre in my voice that hints at shrill. Wah, wah, wahhhhh, I get back, like in the classroom of Charlie Brown. I have no idea what she's saying but I fake it. Pretend I'm taking notes. Say I'll write the letter, fax documents. The insurance rep says thank you for being patient when I'm not, when I'm bad, the kid with ADD.

***

Tomorrow I'm going to check the house for listening devices. Finish the Christmas cards. Leave two unaddressed empty envelopes in the mailbox, push past healing. Push past healed. Visit 1975. All day. The after. The after my father came home. I can see it on a poster in rainbow swirls. A rocket. "Flyin' High." A rock star's song. I'm going to see what it meant for him to have gone and come home.

***

The Truth About 1975

In 1975 my teacher was Mrs. Byrd. I called Kim Campbell a gorilla for cheating at 4-square. The sun was cracked. I was cracked. My mom and dad were cracked. The moon was the last known shell. The days further and further apart. Spreading from the center of the bang. We didn't *know* what *to do*. When you're deceived and you don't know you're deceived, when you're lost and you don't know you're lost, when you escape and you don't know you've escaped, when you come back and *you don't know* you've come back. *You don't go on.* In other words, I go back to hear it and I don't hear it. I go back to sing it and I don't sing it. I go back to see it and I don't see it. There was nothing, *nothing* going on.

***

Right now I'm at a wall. I want to scrap the whole thing. I guess it has to do with being surveilled. Or thinking I'm being surveilled. Maybe listened to. (Three hang-ups in a row today from an "unknown caller," untraceable, unreturnable.) Do with it what you will: I can see my father darting behind trees, like my mother said he did, just back from overseas. Jumping out of the car on a familiar tree-lined street. He thought someone was watching him when maybe someone was.

Maybe I should visit the CIA. Or maybe I'm treading on dangerous, dangerous ground. Hell, I'm already on dangerous, dangerous ground. Besides, I'll just peruse their gift shop--I'm sure they have a gift shop. And maybe it'll convince my father to talk to me, fly in and out of trees. I've read there are lots of trees. After, I'll go for ice cream. Try to throw them off. Ditch my cone. Go zigzag. Run. Run like hell. The sun filtering through the leaves.

***

Places I've Tried to Live:

Court

Circle

Drive

Avenue

Way

Place

Road

Street

Lane

Rotunda (Okay, not "rotunda" but I like saying it. Rotunda, rotunda, rotunda.)

***

Now the phone has given to screeching and clicking in my ear. I think it's my dad. A kind of code. For, "I love you." Or, "You're doing it, kiddo." Or, "Hang in there." Something you can bank on.

***

Healer Appointment Number Four.

Nausea.

And, I want her to put me to sleep. But we talk and move things around. Like organs. And pain. And freakish blood. She laughs, her hands over me. I count the hours I'll have left to fit a possible nap in, the books I've gotta read.

On the way home, perhaps because of the first-in-weeks lift of gray sky, the seven dashes of exhaust above my windshield are a surprise. A Dad Code. But these are celestial, ethereal, so unlike a spy. It's like my dad showing up in wings. It's like talking to my healer. I want to say, let's quiet down and stick to the things I know, like this equals this. Hang-ups and strange letters. Things I can turn into a collage. The picture of a heart with a big fat X on it. Or the intestines stretched out and measured for our awe. At worst, we can get back to letters left in newspapers on the tables of Parisian cafes. French was my grad school language, after all. Overseas was where I was born. In other words, let's make it Healer=Dad. Or, Dad+Healer=Answer. Or, Healer+Dad=ANSWER. Or, Dad=Healer. Let's make it one big bang.

***

When we were young, my sister and I danced on our beds to the 45s my mom and dad bought us. Sometimes one of our parents' friends would come down the hall and peer through our half-closed door. We'd fall down fast. Our music to their music--jazz, low. These were the days after the CIA. These were the days of a trial on TV, the people in the spotlight remotely familiar. If you put your fingers under the door in a house, it looks like they've been cut off. If you tell a story and say it's a story, no one knows whether or not to believe. These were the days we had a backyard with woods, a path, a dry river, a bridge of trees. Here's how a family grieves: it knows to feed itself quietly in shifts. This one up at night. This one is morning. This one drives the car down a highway toward school, she's all grown up, after it's over, she's gone, he's gone, they're all gone, a million miles away. The people of their countries strewn in the street. Like lovers, doubling over, arms outstretched, they fell down. Music of the bars in the background. Rattatatat. Rattatatat. The shadows of blown open doors.

***

If you take all the little airports in the world. And from them, you take all the ones in darkness. And from them, all the ones under a light rain. And from them, all the ones with a linoleum floor, and from them, all the ones with a white cement lawn, and from them, all the ones with a family, a father, a mother, and two little girls, the girls in dresses, holding the hands of their mother and father, outside the small airport, in the warm wet wind, walking and looking for a nearby cab or hotel, you'll have my airport, my exact one, somewhere overseas, sometime in the mid 60s. My father in a suit. My mother wearing a small round hat. My sister and I with our long light brown hair. Sleepy but listening. Aware. Headed to or out of another country. Headed in darkness and warmth with witnesses to a hotel's light, for the night. Gold carpet. Lamplight. A late dinner wheeled in. Covered plates. Warm bread. Juice. So we can sleep, under watch, so we can keep this memory, and what we'll never know about it, to ourselves, as our own. So we can grow up and borrow lives that aren't ours, my sister a professor, me a writer, my father dead, my mother on to remarry, so we can bargain for what we were given, the fascination of being loved by a man we could never possibly know, and the fascination of remembering a childhood among others we could never possibly touch, and a fascination of being born into a country we'd never be allowed to be citizens of, the records lost or disjointed or troubling if we'd try to account for them. Be happy, my sister and I tell ourselves, our father gone. Be happy, we try to, calling each other daily, reeling from our births in a clinic in an African village near an embassy long ago dismantled by angry, angry mobs. Our mother stumbling home after both our births, her own long buried, her own near normal life forgotten, her children and her husband her only witnesses, to what she could no longer describe. The dead in the street, and the ways of the men whose wives she befriended, whose children she would help love, until they were gone, they were all gone, or dead or had chosen to try and forget. Because it had to be enough. That we were born and were alive and went on.

***

What I Do Without My Father

Miss people I've never known.
Dream of war rising from my home.
Sleep on planes.
Speak less.
Live to be unknown.

***

I ask my mother what happened to our dog. It was a dog we had, black, medium sized, when we were in Nepal. She becomes troubled. Something about a friend or he died. She has called me to tell me she's found my immunization record from the time we were in Katmandu. I ask her for the doctor's name. Dr. Damm, she says, spelling it, laughing. "He was Napalese?" I ask. No, he worked with the embassy, she says. I go no further because I'm always disappointed. It's not like she doesn't want to remember but I know that her answers after the usual initial ones get, well, confusing. And she seems to just brush so many things off as if they are unremarkable. For instance, we were robbed days before leaving Nepal. Our house ransacked. "Did they find out who did it?" I had asked, horrified. No answer. Then, no. "Was there an investigation? What did they take?" My mother knows nothing. Soon after, my first memory would take place. My mother having been medicated and whisked off, having suffered what someone termed as a nervous breakdown, my sister and I flew on a plane with my father. My memory? Spitting up into his large hand. But the details. "Mom, what did they medicate you with?" Unknown. "Mom, How did you get back to the states?" *They* flew a doctor from the U.S. to fly back with me. "But who was he? Did you ever see him again? Who arranged this? Who is *they*?" Here, things fall off: I don't remember. I was hospitalized shortly after in D.C., she says. "What hospital?" I don't know. Johns Hopkins? "Mom, that's Baltimore." I don't know. I don't know. In my mind I'm screaming. "They FLEW a doctor to accompany you home? What were your symptoms? What lead up to this? Mom? Mom?" Still, there are few answers.

Once she offered, Well, I was having panic attacks. The first one when I saw a body burning on the street, near a river, a funeral. The body moved. The hands. Another when I flew with some of the other wives down to India in a small plane. You know. Stuff like that. As if I do. And, They said I'd be on medication the rest of my life. "But, Mom," I say, "Anybody would have had panic attacks given your circumstances. Why did they say you had a nervous breakdown? What was your diagnosis? How long were you in the hospital? What did you do?" More nebulous answers. "It's raining now," I tell her and open a window. My mother's voice trails off.

Like their dog tags, my father would tell me, were placed in the mouths of the dead, this is a record for what remains. My Sunday clue. My night clue. My clue of the week, for all I know. *Damn*. Dr. Damm. Dammy Boy. Oh, Dammy Boy....Where are you now, having administered shots to the children of the embassy, of the CIA? My Dammy. My Dr. Damm. I'm troubled, man. I wanna know, what else did you do?

***

A statue of my father's favorite Indian goddess, Kali, we acquired in Nepal. He took it each time he moved, finally, away from us, his family, to Florida, in the late 70s. It resurfaced in the Midwest, in his apartment, that he shared with his girlfriend Ann. And after my father died, Ann gave it to my brother, born seven years after we were home into a time of mistake and confusion and fog. Your dad loved that thing, Ann would say, referring to the statue. Black and iron, the many goddess arms splaying out mythic and strong at her sides. The progeny of a man who quietly took on someone else's rage. When the slow downward spiral of his life became acute. And predictable. He drank too much and his brothers and sister would approach my grandparents, his parents, saying, What are you going to do? My grandparents would make a slow drive out for cocktails, take our, their grandchildren's pictures, pet the dog, and survey things from the exotically furnished living room. We were fine, they reasoned, until my father left, for a state surrounded by ocean on three of its four sides.

***

Two nights ago I saw myself standing in a brook with large smooth protruding stones. I'm not sure, now, what more of the scenario there is, whether it was about getting across and who was there. A shadowy figure or two. Yesterday I got a phone call about a meeting from a woman I don't know. She said, You know, we'll meet at so-and-so's house on Stony Brook. I didn't recognize the other woman's name either and I'd never heard of Stony Brook. She spoke as if it were all familiar to me and I familiar to her. When things like this happen in movies, when things like this happen in literature, when things like this happen in gardens behind stone walls, I understand. This is a sign, I tell the character, the narrator. This is what you've been given. Pick up the phone, follow the road.

***

Today is a terrible pain day. I want to crawl back in bed but I can't. Instead I just make it from couch to car to chair. Last night there was a death on a familiar road. I heard it. I heard it. I heard Stony Brook. On the news. Glass like a river. Blood like a stone. I take this as a terrible clue. One I can't shatter. A life and a clue. I say what doesn't matter is pain.

***

To Do

X   Read again the one unclassified CIA document I was able to access that is linked to my father's name because I still don't understand it and there are so many blacked out parts and nowhere does my father's name appear except that this document always comes up when I search my father's exact name on the CIA's unclassified document website and same for the NSA and same for the various other sites linked to secret institutions, the same document, one document, surfaces over and over again.

> It's typed.
> It's 122 pages long.
> Soviets and weapons.
> Blacked out names.
> It's dated August 1, 1974.
> I'm almost asleep.
> There's a purple light coming from my father's flickering TV.
> There's a purple light coming from my mother's shadow down the hall.
> They are bruised, my mother and my father.
> I already know this.
> I know this.
> I already know they've witnessed more than the likes of me.

***

There were two buildings. Sidewalks travel from below them, up. In the house on the left is plush carpet and a desk near the front door where you had to sign in. The house on the right held the patients who had the seeming freedom to wander outside on the grass. In robes. Both the carpet and the grass worn into a path.

***

It feels like hovering over the ground. It feels like living, to me. Being told there are no memories. Being told I was golden for not wanting to know. Because I know. I know. The truth is hung in the hall like a mirror. The truth is done like a portrait long ago. The truth is what my father could not say or tell us, but what, if we can remember it, we will be.

***

I can see the windows of the car streaming with rain, on the way there. Field after field of broken stalks. When we arrived we'd get busy walking around. Checking on things. Broken windows or the busted up patio. My father would cook for us. We'd sleep in. There was a TV that would get one channel, all fuzzy. Out front a tiny yard. A gravel driveway that led to a gravel road. I remember the tall grasses of the fields surrounding it, fields going fallow, fields leading to timber. You won't disappoint me, he'd reassure us, my sister, brother and me, before he'd leave, the weekend over. My father knew he was hurt. He knew there were people behind him, hurt. He knew he had to live out his days like that. The bargain had been made.

***

I think of my dad's chain smoking as a background to his thoughts: that the streets made a grid in the country I was born to, that the grid was a map for guerrillas, that the map was a gift of the world.

***

Latest Research Results:

My birth date is sometimes given as November 14, 1964, and sometimes November 16, 1964.

I was vaccinated for Yellow Fever in October of 1970, which would mean I was out of the country years after I was told I was not.

The President's Council on Bioethics has determined that "erasing memories risks undermining a person's true identity."

NDE means near death experience. NDE's are so common now there are many documented accounts of tunnels and bright lights, angels, flying, stars. NDE's are so popular they've become practical and acceptable to much of the mainstream, whether we believe they are caused by endorphins or god. NDE's mean life after death, outer-body, universal awareness. They mean heartache for those of us who feel we've almost died, but have no memory of it.

"Trauma," Dr. van der Kolk, prof of psychiatry at Boston U, writes, "is stored in bodily states and physical patterns. . . ."

My heart has an irregular rhythm, which means it palpitates, skips beats, flutters, wriggles as if caught on a line.

Listening devices in the 60s were planted in shoes.

Messages were transported in silver dollars.

My sister and I had a doll house that folded up and was held shut with a metal clasp. In the center was a staircase. On the second floor there were two rooms. A parents bedroom and a kids bedroom, decorated accordingly. Our house was so light we could carry it anywhere.

***

In Nepal, my mother told us, we had a locked wrought iron
        gate.
In Liberia, my mother told us,
women carried their belongings on their heads.
Like their wash.
I remember the gate.
The cement steps
inside. Our wash
spinning
on the line
in the wind. Looking out
from a window
above, I was singing.
My father gone.
My father gone.
My father gone.
To make him tell us
everything.

***

On the land of our second house, there were four ponds. A deep pond; a pond filled by a creek; a shallow, muddy pond; and a still, round pond. My father's ponds. There was the pond with the turtle. The pond with the snake. The pond with the flowing water. And the pond with the hoof prints around it.

***

Prayer

Make me feel better.
Give me a way out.
Make this whole and real and good.
Make this so much more than a dream.
Make my people in this story want to sing.
Make my family in this story want to come back.
Make the love in this story always.
And make it done.
Make it uncovered.
Make it crystal clear.
Make it always.
And forever.
And make me whole.
Make me done and whole.
Make me weep with relief when I'm done.
And make me move on then, satisfied.
Make it all better.
And make it an answer for someone else too.
Make it an answer for someone else too.

***

Today my healer healed me. And she said I was moving on. I tried to get her to tell me if I'm on the right path. I sent the question to her telepathically. I'm not sure if she heard but she didn't answer. Maybe because she thinks it's a given. I get that sense. I'm on the path I'm on. Period. It's all the same. My healer said I'd been sketching. Of course she's right. I've been sketching coins and shoes. My healer said I used to face the pain in my body as deaths. She said now I'm looking at the pain as lives. "One person's presence can determine the fate of so many," I tell her. Telepathically. Easy for you to say, she says back and laughs. But she knows what I mean. We both know what I mean.

***

A CIA FOIA rep called today and said two weeks. He said I'd have my father's file in two weeks.

Lucid coast
and song.
Lucid airplane,
lucid jungle,
lucid hospital all along.
Lucid mother.
Lucid father,
lucid country that I must have loved.
Lucid mirror,
lucid shoe,
lucid, lucid love.
Lucid, lucid love.

***

Notes:

St. Elizabeth's Hospital, where the poet, Ezra Pound, was put away, is in D.C. Maybe Mom stayed there?

The letter I got from the CIA promising they'd get back to me about Dad's time working for them had a wide piece of packing tape over the seal. I don't know if this is standard procedure or if the guy just didn't want to lick the envelope and that's the kind of tape he had on his desk.

Something like this could make you crazy, go crazy, dealing with the CIA and trying to BELIEVE their promises. I mean, who are we kidding? Maybe it goes on like this for years. Maybe that's the point, to lose your mind in the process. Maybe *I'll* wind up in St. Elizabeth's in D.C.

And by the way, what IS a nervous breakdown? Back then? Now? Let's think about giving it some parameters. Note to self: Look into "nervous breakdown."

Only one other time did I get something in the mail I was really worried about opening (as I imagine I'll feel when Dad's "file" finally comes). Copies of some drafts of Sylvia Plath's poems held at Smith College. Go figure. It's that I wanted to be ready for them. Have my desk (meaning my life) cleared so I could dive in. Do the work I'd need to do.

I feel like I'm constantly being pulled up and up out of sleep by my shoulders. I'm half startled, my heart fluttering. I say, Wha? What? And then fall back only to have it happen again and again, like some kind of low-key torture. And when I'm fully awake I can feel it, the same kind of thing, needling me, but it's more like a presence, disaster.

***

I look up nervous breakdown in the dictionary. In my mind it requires some kind of public display. Like on TV. Think Mariah Carey or Mary Hartman. A circumstance where you wind up losing it on national television. A before and after. One day you are just going along in an insane situation with an insane mind and then you end up taking off your clothes on national television or giggling uncontrollably and saying incoherent and/or bizarre things while you sort of concave into a human soft pile. So I'm not sure what I mean when I say that Mom had a nervous breakdown. Hers wasn't broadcast. What I ultimately imagine is that she sort of zoned out, became incapacitated. That the will to pick up one's foot and walk just went. My favorite dictionary doesn't shed much more light with its vague offering: "a severe or incapacitating emotional disorder." Maybe that's why people don't use the term so much anymore.

***

Note: Get up the nerve to ask Mom if St. Elizabeth's, a government hospital for the insane, rings a bell. Just out of the blue: Hey, Mom, ever heard of . . . ? Or, What do you think of a hospital established by the government for the insane? Or, Did that time you worked in the library of the state mental hospital bring up any particular memories? Any particular names of any particular places come to you? Or, Mom, how about we go on a little road trip? (Standing out front of St. Elizabeth's): Seem familiar? Having any flashbacks? Okay, maybe this isn't such a good idea. Maybe the answers are given to you and then you can ruin them by going around asking a lot of questions. And what's the difference anyway? A mental hospital is a mental hospital is a mental hospital, right? Especially in the mid 60s. Maybe you just live with the pieces that are handed to you pretty easily. Maybe you just take those scraps and make a collage.

***

Things To Do

Buy poster board.

Research "collage."

***

Note:

Research kinds of packing tape, purposes. CIA linked to packing tape. Messages inherent in kind of packing tape used.

***

Note:

Call Public Information Line at CIA and give them a gentle reminder that it's been two weeks. You know, a nudge. Yeah, *nudge* the CIA. The officer that's been assigned to you. Coax him along. Joke around a little. Say, There's this identity crisis I'm trying to work through and, well, this particular bit of information could SAVE ME FROM HAVING MY OWN LITTLE STAY IN AN INSTITUTION. Then start laughing, like you've made a joke. Heh, heh, heh.

Okay, YOU'RE DEALING WITH THE CIA. THEY COULD CARE LESS ABOUT YOUR PARTICULAR PERSONAL CRISIS. Call them and be matter of fact. Professional: This is a courtesy call. I'm calling to remind you it's been two weeks and I haven't received the *letter*. . . .

***

(So much for letting go.)

***

My research on the collage leads me to nothing more than what we all mostly know. Except that there's been some kind of headway on how to make the stuff adhere. And it's not with packing tape. (Heavy sigh.)

***

Plath's broad letters, her handwriting, were what first struck me. The loops. And the way she scratched things out so that you couldn't see. You can trace the girl in those loops. Poppies in July and October, the poems. I was never astounded, just affirmed, sleeping for a long time, by the bright orange sun in the window, a manila envelope, open, on the floor.

***

There's some guy holding the envelope that I'm supposed to have, he's running, trying to hand it off, but I can't catch up. That's why I wake so tired. Because I never catch up. It's too damn far.

***

And then there's the local mental hospital's presence always needling me. Tonight one of the two orbs that light the entrance was out. And yesterday a van of patients heading to the store. They unload and travel inside wandering up and down the aisles. And then the guy closest to my age. Long hair. He's thinking I have no idea what it's like. When I do. It's weird looking out from a van like that. You could, most of the time, care less, being seen. There's a freedom to being categorized. It's all you have. That moment. And it's the last thing you want to give up. Especially at night. It's good, that way. Living. In the moment. It's what all the philosophers are after. The guy shuffling ahead of you concentrating on one thing. Wiping down the handle on the cart. So he can wipe clean the person that came before. So he can touch it.

***

My sister and I are shooting emails back and forth doing our Mom's Misnomers Game, when it comes to me. There should be a website, a newsletter, for children of CIA agents. Maybe the newsletter could come inside a donut or something. Anyway, beyond the logistics of its existence, it could be such a release. I've already thought of some titles for articles:

That's *Embassy* Not *Missionary*

Dual Citizenship: Not What It's Cracked Up To Be

What's in a Country? Being Born *Overseas*

***

I imagine someone running into the woods, across the fields, next to the mental hospital, a giant light bulb in his hand. He's whooping it up, yelling out, singing. He stole the bulb so I'd note that there was only one, and it meant something. To hang on. To stand alone in the dark. To yell out. To drive by and look in.

***

In this scene I'm an intern, a med student, and I haven't got a clue. Somehow I've gotten here knowing nothing, yet people treat me as if I'm up to par. The clincher is trying to take the elevator down 20 floors after our first meeting. I'm afraid of elevators. Now I'll be known for what I am: a mental. A dog runs past just before I force myself on. As I take his ragged, dragging leash, the elevator doors close without me.

***

The summer of my freshman year in college I got paid to record kinds of bike racks on campus. Considering the mid-western campus was huge and home to 27,000 students when it was in full swing, I walked a lot to do this job. The residence halls farthest out were only four stories high. There the wind blew wildly and the heat rose from the sidewalks and the dorms, virtually empty, gaped. That summer I knew I'd never go back. I'd learned to do something new. With my colored felt-tip pens and blueprints. Record. See. Record. See.

***

One of my best friends says, Cowboy up. Then another best friend shoots back that she has a hitch in her getalong. I'm twisted up so tight I can't let go enough to laugh. Neither of them know what's going on with me. It's hard to put into words how much you've invested in signs and ghosts and the mail and the CIA. Let's face it, even best friends can draw the line. So I fake laugh, chuckle, breathe in what everyone thinks is my neighbor's cigarette smoke. But I know it's my dad's. That dad. He's back in town. Cloud upon cloud in the air.

***

Night after night, my father would light a fire. Even when it was almost warm. He'd build a house. Line it with paper and sticks. Throw on dust for us. Watch it glow. Purple. Yellow. Green.

***

Our youngest of two, second daughter, says she feels like a crummy country. I'm glad I'm not alone, I tell her. *No, really*, she says, *a country, a crummy country*. It's *universe*, I tell her. Crummy *universe*. She laughs and eventually falls asleep, a country docking at her side. I go back to trying to figure things out. Swim to my own bed through stars.

***

The CIA FOIA rep calls me back. It's a new one. My request is in the *Completion Phase*. Another month. Sure.

***

Laundry piled throughout a bedroom. "Me" sits next to a pile on the bed cradling a phone between her shoulder and ear. Folds laundry. Dryer and washer sounds in the background.

CIA FOIA rep: It's in the final stage.
Me: How many stages are there?
CIA FOIA rep: Laughter.
Me: No, I mean, you know, it's been over a year since I sent in my request. Is there a time frame for each stage? I was just wondering how long this stage usually takes. Like will it be another year?
CIA FOIA rep: Oh, no, maybe, you should have it in around a month.
Me: Oh.
CIA FOIA rep: We've had a lot of requests. We're really backed up.
Me: Thinking: It always comes down to plumbing. Me: talking: Okay, thanks.
CIA FOIA rep: (Sounding even more impossibly normal): Yes, well, good-bye.
Me: Okay, good-bye.

***

Just when I'm getting desperate again, thinking about the labyrinth again, thinking about Miami (long story--my dad, mom, sister and I lived there briefly between overseas trips), she calls me back to say a month. I planned to walk the labyrinth out of desperation or hop a plane, call my mom on my layover and ask where we lived while in Miami, then trek on over there upon landing. But that would be risky. Mom would say something like, The green side. Or, The area with all the tropical flowers. There was a lot of lattice in the yard. A really good breeze. So I'd end up calling out to my dad. Yoo-hoo, Ghost Dad. Hey, over here. Got any CIA clues? We're close to Cuba. Or was this just a good landing place for you and your CIA family between gigs. It was warm? You could go deep sea fishing. Mom could be really, really distracted by all the tropical scents and ocean breeze. I could learn to walk at the beach. And the labyrinth? It's just somewhere, given my bizarre, random, disjointed catholic upbringing, I feel compelled to go. Another place where things might be given back to you whole, when you do it, walk to the center. Since it's cement, a spiral path with no walls, I see myself lying down in the middle under a clear sky and fat sun, kind of like a bull's eye for answers. Answers, come to me, I'll chant. Answers, Come, like I'm calling one of our dogs. Then I'll get up all dizzy and make my way to the car, if not enlightened at least with a better tan. Or at the very least my face rosy. I'll beeline it to the DQ drive thru for my fountain diet Coke. And I'll deserve it. I'll deserve the bubbles and the caffeine. Put in a shot of cherry, I'll sing into the drive thru speaker, my windows down, cars zipping by, everyone seemingly full of zeal, with important or at least determined places to go.

***

I saw it as a horse, but it wasn't a horse. Blood like a bright red balloon, coming from its mouth. "It was just startled," our youngest daughter says. "You spit up blood when you are startled. It's quivering. It will get up and go," she says. I saw it as a horse instead of the deer it was because I'd seen a horse like that before. Or maybe it was a man, a woman, a child, a family, many families, many people, startled to death, thrown down. They weren't people. They were horses, I told myself, I could look them straight in their dead ways. And speak about it, I told myself.

***

I'm reading *The Higher Power of Lucky* before my daughters do. Apparently it's controversial since it contains the word *scrotum*. But my girls've heard the word *scrotum*. Don't kick me in the *scrotum*, their dad will sometimes say, while they all wrestle. The book must be good, I figure, if some parents are calling for it to be pulled off school library shelves. It must say something more important than *scrotum*, if some parents are afraid. Heads up, I'll say, chucking it into one or the other's room. You won't be disappointed. Hey, try this, I'll offer, holding out *The View from the Cherry Tree.* It'll knock your socks off, I'll mention, laying *The Changeling* on one or the other's bed. It's art. Read it, I'll add, over my shoulder, having left *Mystery of the Third Twin* on a pillow. Daughter one, the oldest, usually nods her head in acknowledgment. Daughter two, the youngest, more often than not, sighs heavily. (She's tired of being bossed.) My own mother let us get as many books as we wanted at the library. More. If we'd go past the limit, we'd use each other's cards. All three of us, my mother, sister, me, under teetering piles. She'd happily smack her gum while paying our past due fines. Let us read all night. No one ever got in trouble for lost books. Books left on planes.

***

I run out of gas in the elementary school parking lot. My sister happens to have a container of gas. I reach her on my cell phone which shows one bar of battery left. I feel like I have a bull's eye on my head, I say. We laugh our heads off. That's what we say, Laugh your head off. My sister has the wide bright face of an apple. Big eyes. We peel back to the inner core. Dad rolled up paper to make a funnel, I tell her. She grabs a magazine and rips it in half. And hands it to me.

***

I send out an email to my three close friends from high school. I've been sick for the last two days. When I get sick, my throat tends to rage and it feels like someone is running a blade up and down my limbs. I say in the email, Don't leave me, don't give up on me, no matter how bad it gets. They have no idea what I'm talking about. I send it out around 3 a.m. between doses of ibuprofen. My head spins, my muscles feel as though someone is trying to split them open like filets. When sick in the past, like a drunk, I've made bizarre apologetic phone calls, written wills and testaments. So the email comes as no real surprise to my friends. They figure I'm onto a major sinus infection and put in a call to my husband. Check on her. She's at it again. Unplug the computer. Hide the phone. And it's a good thing. Because I don't know how much more I can take. My body is caving like a coward. I want my life back, I mumble incoherently, as my husband tucks me in. I just want to know who I am. He nods his head apologetically. Whisks off to check the Sent File.

***

There's a write-up in the Sunday *Washington Post* about Howard Hunt, one of the Watergate burglars, and how he also claimed to have been approached by rogue CIA agents plotting to kill President Kennedy in 1963. According to the *Post*, Hunt was always suspected, himself, as being sympathetic with "his Cuban exile friends' hatred of Kennedy, who refused to provide air cover to rescue the 1961 Bay of Pigs invasion" that Hunt helped organize. I try a new tactic with Mom since we lived in Miami around that time. I email her. *Mom, **when** did we live in Miami?* I get an indirect response. "It was Coral Gables." (South Miami.) And, "Twice. Once when I was pregnant with your sister," in that I wasn't born yet. "And once when we had both of you." If I'm right, it would have been 63 the first time. I wonder how many CIA agents hung out in Miami around then. I wonder if my father knew or got wind of the supposed Kennedy plot before, during or after. And I wonder why, otherwise, we were in Miami. It may have been a sort of layover between missions. If my sister was about to be born, they were headed to Africa. Our second stay isn't one I can be as sure about. I know an apartment was secured for us each time so the stays were longer than vacations, but other than that I know nothing. I shoot an email back and ask what years. I don't get an answer.

***

Left-handed in a catholic school was a bad, bad thing. Think of it as a trick, I told myself, because it made me feel so much pain. When I learned why Dad was ambidextrous. *You know he was beaten to get like that*, I tell my husband, between sobs. *But he survived. He learned to write with both hands.* And that's the point, isn't it? He didn't give one thing up for another.

***

Grandpa, I tell our girls, was just a kid, when he dropped out of college and joined the army. With his baby face. Blue eyes. From his childhood home, a craftsmanish mansion built by his dad, my grandfather, for his wife, their great grandmother, on Lover's Lane, set back from the road at the top of a long curving drive, the plaster inside imported, still wet when it arrived, he, the wild child, took off toward stifling humidity one of my daughters describes as blurry air. God, it was hot, Dad would say, the air conditioner wheezing in the background, smoke spilling out of his ash tray. Silence encroaching upon us in the beautifully furnished room.

***

Our neighborhood, where we finally settled, was an oval where, at the top, the country club stood. The country club's craftsmanish architecture dark and woody much like the house my grandfather built for my grandmother. Its pool Olympic and shaped like an L. Its tennis courts hot under the sun, deserted the long midwestern winters, rainy cool springs and falls. Its golf course with its swells of closely cropped grass. That at night you could run. Under stars. The sand pits empty, the greens smooth and soft as blankets. The place treeless and wide. Mine. I just had to cross from my yard. And run. Until I was forgiven. Of everything I was. Of everything.

***

I see two images before waking. One is of a beach house that is both beautiful and eerie/old. It is pretty empty. Except in one upstairs room, very bright with light from the beach/ocean, is a doll. Maybe in a rocking chair. In the other image, I see dark wood stairs going up many flights. If you look up, you can see many flights at once. You can hear footsteps. Footsteps of a man, I think. I think it's an empty building also. There's a woman chasing him, trying to see who the man is, if it's who she thinks it is. She's out of breath, panting. I think that woman is me.

***

When I was eight or nine, we'd sometimes ride out to the cabin of friends on weekends. The place was on a river. High up on bluffs. All day on Saturday their youngest girls and my sister and I would play along the banks. Keeping as our landmark the one bridge within walking distance. Decrepit. I used to hold my breath when we crossed it in our car, hoping we wouldn't fall on the mud flats below. You could hear the wood slats shifting beneath our tires. As if releasing. My father smoked his cigarette all the way across. And drank. My mother sewed. We must have held onto the dog or dared ourselves to look below. The railing, two narrow bands of rust. Then we were across. It was difficult to breathe. The thick foliage along the banks. The nettles and blooming grass. The sad fat frogs carrying their children on their backs. The mosquitoes and fire pits and hazy heat. The drive home.

***

I see *The Good Shepherd*, the movie about the inception of the CIA and some of its internal events up to the Cold War. Here's what they got right. CIA agents are afflicted; wives of CIA agents are distressed; kids of CIA agents are sad;
    it's a legacy.

Spies can be poets; Poets can be spies.

***

Our youngest hates school. Because it's an institution? I say. It's political? She stares at me blankly. You are surrounded by conservatives? The people that conform the most succeed? Because we know standardized tests don't really test anything? Some days you feel like you could leap out of your skin because there are so many subliminal messages from the Far Right? She rolls her eyes. I try being more specific. PE? She falls back on her bed as if exhausted. Look, I offer, trying to hone in on her hardships with friends and crabby teachers and injustices, bullies and drudgery and antiquated teaching practices. We're all undercover, I say. You're the granddaughter of a covert man. A spy. You are special in that way. Act, I say, like it's normal. Act, I say, like it all makes sense. Act, I say, like your biggest goal in life is to get an A. Act, I say, like the most important thing to you is to behave. Then just go on secretly with who you are, bide your time, while you learn what there is to learn. I'm still learning, I tell her. The point, I say, Well, for me, you are one of the points. No pressure, I add. I was one of the points for your grandfather. The other points will make themselves known but you have to *do it,* I say. You have to immerse yourself, in your case, in the world of a ten-year-old kid. And get on with it. Ohhhhh-kkaaaaayyyyy, she sighs, as if I've asked her to clean her room or walk the dog. And I can't believe it. I'm off the hook. Until tomorrow morning. The ride to school which should prove harrowing. I extricate myself from her bed, its blankets and stuffed animals, sketch pads and books, thinking there is no way out of this.

***

In high school I found Sylvia Plath's autobiographical novel, *The Bell Jar*. After reading it, I was almost aloft, like the rug a ghost lifts off the floor or a washed plate pulled out of the sink into air.

***

Our youngest wants to go to Rhymes and Reasons, a daycare, after school. She says they have a rock climbing wall, and there she won't be worried about the house burning down. Her other plan is that we adopt. No babies. A sixteen year old who can drive her around. This, she says, will keep her mind occupied. Even if the teenager is agreeable, I say, you're putting all your eggs in one basket, thinking this will cure your worries. I go through them. It's not tornado season and they are rare here anyway. We're not in a fire zone or in a drought. We have working smoke alarms and our house's electrical has been inspected. . . . In three minutes, she's asleep. I crawl from her bed carefully, walk past the lamp with its glowing fish, swimming steadily past their back light in an even crawl, slip on my shoes, vow to make a plan for Monday, the week. How to keep this family afloat. Eating right and sleeping. I check our other daughter. Turn out her light. Fold laundry. Watch the rain bounce and run along the back deck, my husband out, in front of the TV. News of war on low, citizens of the world running past. Guns or blankets or clothes or food or children on their backs.

***

My sister has a "bright spot" on her brain. According to the doctor, it means nothing other than it has been linked to migraines. Somewhere there is a list of people with bright spots on their brains, I say. My sister's connected. She's divine. I see it clearly. She's been touched by the hand of god. Really. I mean this. I've always known this about my sister. She can stand up to a bully and *win,* and she's not a bully. I remember the *first* time. Dad, a few months home, was tucked away in his home office, smoking cigarettes like they were going out of style. Mom was cleaning or cooking or sewing and talking on the phone. "*She* is my *sister*," my sister said, stepping in front of me, telling the bully with a dead snake or lizard or fish in his hand, the bully moving the animal like it's alive. "And that thing in your hand is dead. D-E-A-D, dead. You can't scare us!" The bully shrinks. He's a Shrinky Dink, that bully. Poof. He's gone.

***

I have to do research, our youngest announces, when she gets home from school. One of her favorite topics to worry about. We're studying tornadoes, she says. They gave us a website. You know, I need to find out stuff like where tornadoes occur, how many people were killed last year, how many people injured, what states have the most tornadoes. "Great," I say. "You sure? Not another topic?" But she's resolute. Stony. She wants to get it done. Later, in the car, she announces Hawaii's never had one. "One what?" I say. They don't have tornadoes there, she says. *What the heck?* says my sister later from her hospital bed where they are making her lie flat for 24 hours. *How many killed? The kid is in fourth grade!* I can see her shouting at the ceiling, distracted, slightly, while she waits. The bright spot a halo on her gorgeous brain.

***

Today

>Don't eat any more cherry pie
>Think about the symbolic connection of
>impatience and impatiens
>Rail against the establishment
>Don't get discouraged
>Don't get discouraged
>Try not to get discouraged
>Get past getting discouraged
>Make a coherent list

***

I just did a tally of swear words I frequently use. I think I need to renegotiate. I think I need to reconsider. I rely too much on the standards. They're losing their punch. Of course I can't use them when I really need to, like when I'm on the phone with the CIA FOIA people: WHERE THE FUCK IS THE INFO I REQUESTED? ANYBODY? ARE YOU FUCKING LISTENING? DOES ANYONE THERE HAVE A FUCKING BRAIN? IS ANYONE THERE CAPABLE OF RECOGNIZING UTTER FUCKING DESPERATION? DOES ANYONE KNOW HOW THE FUCK LONG I'VE BEEN PATIENT? Like I said, "punchy" doesn't seem to be where I'm headed.

***

Monday

X	Feel completely deluded, that I'll never have enough genius to figure this out, that I'm somehow just bad, unequipped, unpopular, a social misfit

Write the CIA and explain that the information I requested about my dad is no longer necessary. Say that, being my father's daughter, I know all there is to know. Say, But you already knew that, didn't you? Say it in French, N'est-ce pas?

Drop off old clothes

Windex

X	Write

***

I love as if there is a country between us to get across. As if there is tragedy we just escaped. As if the past three days is not a deluge of cardinals. The lighter red brown of the females and the bright red of the males. And, with the backdrop of an achy blue sky, a soaring tall twisted overgrown lilac bush, turned dying tree in an old farmhouse yard. So twisted upon itself and half of it dead, the color of ash, but within huge lilac blooms. On the opposite side of the road I'm on, turned south while I'm headed north.   But people were shot in my dreams.

***

I'm so hungry and tired and delirious and utterly and impossibly and absolutely and joyfully resolved to defeat, I say, giggling and weepy and completely and deliriously happy, I say, I could eat the dashboard, the countertop, napkins, the table. I could eat the chair, the sidewalk, vinyl, the plate. I could eat the steering wheel, the tires, the hood of the car, that telephone pole, the traffic light, the fixtures, the bar. I could eat the lamps, the chandelier, the door. Bring me anything and I will eat it whole. And I won't look back.

***

Then comes the Led Zeppelin song, what *is* it?, and when we get home our youngest touches, one at a time, with purpose, the backs of both our hands, as if she is blessing us or fixing us to the earth, the garage where we stand waiting for her to put away her scooter while our oldest has her hand on the door, waiting, having just before we got home, called us on the cell to say the youngest wanted to go outside and she'd told her to come in because it was getting dark and would we back her up because she was worried about her sister and we say, yes, you're in charge and I don't know where to go but the song was huge, at the end of a warm, warm, warm day, except that I almost wrote *war*, *war* day, and I'm finally warm, till we get in the house where the air is on, blowing, but I think at least my skin smells good from the sweet lotion and the girls are happy, for the moment, being that we've brought dinner, and the dogs and all the girls' pets, and all of it, but back and back to the song, that song, the acousticness of it, the hollowness of it, the haunting and the time, the era, and his voice and us and how we didn't know each other yet but appreciated the same things and were trying to get away from something, except they were different things, all of that and how there were good times I had forgotten about when I began this search because it was a bad time when I began it and how I keep trying to get back to it and go deep, each time, but it's so hard because, no, I don't know, I lose it, or something, and I can't seem to keep it at the forefront and sometimes I'm just so pissed off and don't know how to forgive people for what they've done to other people and my dad and my sister and my mother and my brother and me, and my dad who is dead now so I just don't know how. I just don't know how. I just don't know how to go on. Except that my husband sings to the song in the car, he *sings* perfectly, sexy, beautiful, like he is, to the song.

***

My sister, math education guru, calls and doesn't leave a message. It's too late for me to call back. She is probably up preparing for one of her workshops. And wanted to talk while she hauled up bins of brightly colored blocks from her basement. Tomorrow she'll inform a bunch of new teachers how to teach math hands-on. So the kids will really get it. So they'll be loud and busy and laughing. So they'll sing. Math is all about patterns, she'll say. While her daughters were getting the pattern concept, I was having mine hoist their own hardback dictionaries onto their beds for reference. Just in case. This is a dictionary, I'd say to them, when they were so young. Words are inside. You can look them up. It's fun, I'd add weakly. "Okay," they'd say, in unison, while standing on them, using them as landings for their toy airplanes, foundations for their blocks, floors for their doll furniture. How they accepted what I had to give. It seems such a miracle. Like my father. Leaving us to come home.

***

We are sitting in a crowd, mostly families, waiting for our daughter's band concert to begin, and then I see this guy walking by, making his way toward his family, and I wonder what secret he's got, until I think, No way, that guy doesn't have a secret, he looks too normal I'm just looking for stuff and besides that's so cliché to think everybody's got a secret and then I think that's so cliché to think he looks too normal to have a secret. And then the concert begins. And then it's over. And then our daughter runs up and asks if we can go get ice cream to celebrate and soon we are taking two of her friends too and outside the ice cream place they are running around screaming so that when we get home much later I lie down on the bed right on top of books and papers and notes and notes to myself about this, my dad, and everything, and then our daughter comes in and says, "Can you lie down with me, I'm scared," and I say, I can't move, can you go get your dad. And she does.

***

I see myself with tape over my mouth. Then I see myself as a kid on a field trip outside a museum. I'm eating my sandwich, sitting on grass, wondering when this thing is going to be over. Back to the tape. It's not a flashback or anything. I don't remember it or anything. I just see myself that way for a minute. I can feel the tape on my mouth and then I wonder why you couldn't just open your mouth pulling loose the tape even if your hands were bound and I think I should try it except that my hands won't be bound I'll just not use my hands but then I think, no, that is sick so I'm just left with the image and the feeling and then I remind myself not to get so weird about everything and then I just want to get away from here, walk on a beach, or get some sleep before my daughter wakes up. And then I remember the dusty gift shop inside the museum, an old lady behind the counter counting out my coins and how museum gift shops, always packed with kids on my daughters' field trips, are a whole lot more than they were then. Crazy, spinning.

***

I tell myself I'm going to better concentrate on my writing. And then my dreams turn color. Velvet stairs. Cupolas and tiled floors. Courtyards and mossy bricks. Porticos. Dormers. A moon. The glow and shine of copper, an inlaid wood floor. Sconce light and lamp light. Glass doors.

***

I never knew Patrick nor did my husband but we go to his memorial service because my husband works with his mom. Patrick's body was found in the Hudson. The hope was that he was following a band. That he'd left college for a weekend to see friends in New York and changed his mind. After we go to the memorial service, I read a poem he had written and through a series of coincidences and other circumstances I meet one of his writing teachers. The poem is good. The picture of Patrick in the paper is gorgeous. Not knowing what else to do, my husband and I give each of his family members journals. I think journals are for secrets. Maybe Patrick's family members can write his down. Maybe it'll help them go on. Just to write, I think Patrick had a secret. Like you identify. Like this is how you go on.

***

I call my mom. I'm so sick it feels like someone is trying to filet my muscles, I say, sneezing. She tells me about her car. She tells me she's cleaned the house. She's getting old. And she's alone. I hang up the phone. I clip and count thousands of UPC's for our daughters' schools. I send them off. I read and memorize the signs for stroke. I tell my sister when she makes fun of my volunteer job clipping UPC's collected by the girls' schools that she just likes to boss people around. If you volunteer and it doesn't involve a microphone and bossing you're not in, I say. She laughs out loud. I embrace that moment with everything I've got. Then after the girls are asleep, I throw myself in the car and drive. And cry. I'm going to say more, I say, about the truth. *I'm going to try, I'm going to try, I'm going to try.* I'm going to use the truth as a weapon. A plow. A blade. Seeds. Facts: 1. My father worked for the CIA. 2. He never divulged his secrets. 3. His secrets have informed my life. 4. His secrets that I do not know. 5. There is probably horror behind those secrets. 6. It is not possible to heal from such horror. 7. It is only possible to go on.

***

I know I'm making choices that shut people out. But I have to, to find my father, before he's totally gone. You're okay with this, kid? he says to me. "Of course I'm not okay, Dad," I say to him. "Of course not. I haven't been myself for a long time."

***

I call my sister from a major department store. Between panic attacks. "Why are you making me do this?" I say. What? she says. "Go to the store." She laughs. "I hate this," I say. I know, she says. Hang tight. You'll get through. "There are too many people here," I whine. "I'm overwhelmed." Your kids have to eat, she says. They need shampoo.

***

I call our oldest who is camping with the family of one of her friends. I get mostly monosyllabic answers to my questions. How are you? "fine." How's it going. "fine." Did you sleep well? "yes." What are you doing. "eating." Is your arm hanging from your body by threads? "nope." Are you ready to throw yourself into the lake you're so despondent and miss us so much? "nope." Are you drinking enough water? "yep." Wearing sunscreen? "yep." Will you call me if you want to talk. "yep." Click. This is the daughter who at the age of 12 set the rules for her independence. Leave Me Alone. (Except when I need you. And, boy, will I need you.) Periods of silence followed by periods of wanting to process every detail of her day with me and only me, her mother. This is the girl who at the age of eight said she was going vegan and the thought of eating meat disgusted her. "How COULD we," she said, stamping her foot. Who promptly joined PETA at age 11 and refused to touch, sit on, or wear leather. "Is that leather?" she'll ask me, panic on her face. No, I'll say, you're safe. This is the daughter who despite her periodic and complete avoidance of her immediate family has a heart big enough to house all the animals of the world. Every one. Who has not faltered, questioned, or looked back since her decision five years ago. This is a girl who knows her truth. I wish I knew the same.

***

At the middle school 10 military jets fly overhead. An eighth grader runs inside yelling, They're bombing us, they're bombing us. I call my sister. Her machine picks up. "I have a major announcement to make," I say loudly. I hear her on the line panting. *There's a group of people here*, she says in an emphatic whisper. *I'll call you back.* When she does I can't remember what I was going to say. "I've perfected my swan dive? I can now make crepe suzettes? I've gone blonde?" Later I clip an article out of the paper. "Emergency Preparedness: The First Three Days." I vow to stockpile and double up. My sister's family, mine. Then I say to no one, but as if there's a target, My sister helped me escape.

***

I reread the article on emergency preparedness and take note. Rain gear. We need rain gear. We also need coins. For plugging into smashed vending machines for stale crackers and Moon Pies? I think. Why not just tip the machines over? You anarchist, I think. Criminal. Looter. The girls and my husband shaking their heads. All geared up and standing behind me in their raincoats.

***

Fear no art, I say to our oldest as she's getting out of the car for school. "Yep," she says, acting like she didn't really hear my instructions. Or that this is the easiest way to get out of the car quickly. After all, there are other kids within earshot. I learned long ago not to say, I love you, or, Good-bye, Beautiful. So this is my new tactic. I leave her. I go to the gas station. I pull out and I'm hit with the sun. A fire ball. Popsicle orange.

***

One of the girls opens up a small package of tiny plastic shoes. I find a pink high heel by the computer. A tiny tennis shoe by a living room vent. A brown oxford on a stair. My sister calls. I'm staring at the shoes. "What?" I say. She laughs. Wassup? she says. Now I laugh. "I'm staring at a pile of shoes," I say. She understands.

***

I put the shoes in a jar. Along with a penny, a button, and some little number tiles. A 5, a 4, and a 3. I stay up all night packing us for Maine. I email my sister I'm in a "stubor" (Mom's pronunciation of stupor). I decide Henry Kissinger is a war criminal even though he doesn't know it. I wait for the last load of laundry to dry. I lie down. I give up on the laundry. I listen to the moon. I decide if Henry Kissinger is partly responsible for what happened to my father and what happened to my family and what happened to me. I decide I'm thirsty. I stumble toward water. I fall down. I'm numb. I want to determine why. Then I remember I'm just so tired. I say it, I'm just so tired. I'm just so tired.

***

In Maine we find loads of sea glass. I get sick on clams. A train passes through and I tell its sound, Help me remember what I do not know. I'm just waking up, train, I say. Go backwards. But it's too late, the sound is gone.

***

Across the dark, I take our youngest's hand. I'm not going to talk now, I say. After I tell her it won't always be this way. After she brightens and then it falls away. In her journal she's drawn a picture of her ideal school. A glass top so you can see the sky. A picture of van Gogh as a boy. Brimming with ideas. And pain. It all turns out all right, I say, breaking my silence. "I know," she says. "But I don't want to have to wait."

***

I interrupt Mom on her way to her weightlifting class. "We've had a break in the heat," she says. "I had all the windows open last night for the breeze." I'm lonely, I say. We're at the pool, I tell her. When we get home, I pile everything on our bed that has to be done. There's no room for sleeping. I water the flowers. You are goodness, I say to the flowers. Drink. I hang up the beach towels. Feed the dogs. Sweep the floor. You are goodness, dogs, I say, petting them. I fill their water bowls. Drink up, I say. You're so thirsty. I weave my body in among the piles of papers and laundry and suitcases on the bed. I close my eyes. You are goodness. You are goodness. You are goodness, I say.

***

My sister calls from a mosh pit. A what? I yell back. "I'm in a *mosh pit*," she screams. All I can hear is a cacophony of sounds behind her voice. What the heck? I shout, borrowing our daughters' common phrase. "I couldn't get other seats," she hollers. CALL! ME! LATER! I yell. YOU! NEED! TO! PAY! ATTENTION! YOU'RE! GOING! TO! GET! KILLED! When she does call, she says she's got a headache and is lying on the couch. "I just need a night off," she says. "Some peace." Go figure, I say. No more pits, I tell her. Okay, maybe one or two.

***

When the question comes up at the MVA, Have you ever had a driver's license under another name? I falter. A split second, a half a second, so short the clerk doesn't even notice. I do a slapstick of the whole thing in my mind for my sister. I'd been meticulous about the paperwork. The directions here. Something to do while I wait. But none of it works. The question comes as a surprise. The policemen make me nervous. I'm rattled. Abuzz. I try to remember what a lie is. I muddle around in the past. My passport, the tattered beauty, is a revelation to me. And that this is how I began.

***

I'm not able to reach my sister. I give up after four dropped calls. Then I reach my brother-in-law. We consult each other about my sister's latest trip to the dentist. She's swollen, he says in a worried voice, and you know how it is. Pain medication just doesn't work well on her. She needs a double dose. My girls in the background writhing in their suits. From exhaustion and too much sun. I hang up and try to herd them toward the bath. But the going is difficult. There are lots of stops. We make it halfway up the stairs before there's a breakdown. I steel myself and help them toward separate showers. The dogs find places to hide. I stand outside their doors and hand them PJ's and towels and shampoo. "It's okay," I recite, "you're just tired. You need sleep." The answer seems easy enough when I say it, over and over again.

***

All over the world people are looking. Looking, even, for their own arms. It is difficult to believe. But this is one thing I know is true. In the background the sound of laughter. Or like one night. A foreign country. I couldn't see. I couldn't see the faces of my companions. For a long time. I felt the chair, the table. Heard other voices in the distance. But that was all.

***

When I tell other mothers I'm a writer, they invariably look at my shoes. Like my footwear will somehow save me. "She sleeps all day" was my girls' explanation. Enough said for a five year old. Made sense to them. She's up all night writing so "she sleeps all day." If I was standing there, I'd stumble in with "Well, I write at night." Oh, I'd get back. Suspicion. Why can't you write during the day, Lady? they're thinking. While your kids are in school. Because daytime, if you really want to know, I would have offered, drags on. Night flies by. At night I think up great ideas. We need a set of mountain goats, I decide. Because somebody should use the patio furniture. In the local paper, there are pictures of miniature goats in someone's backyard standing happily on glass-topped tables. A tiki bar. And since that's a good idea, why not take in the local scene by joining the county cloggers. My kids will be able to say something else. She sleeps all day and she's a clogger. It's really draining. Clogging.

***

In an interview for a writer in residence position, after I've discovered my job entails convincing kids who don't want to write, to write, I decide to lie. I've never been good at convincing people anything. If you don't want to write, don't write, I'll think. My father worked for the embassies, I say, in answer to her questions about my childhood world travel. It's an old lie. A lie I haven't used in years. But by now I'm exhausted. With the whole damn thing. I don't want this job. "Do you still have ties there?" my interviewer asks. No, I say, lying again. Of course I've got ties. I've got all kinds of ties. But not like the ones she means. Picture me buoyed like a kite in the air. Strings hanging down all over the earth. I'm aloft again. Thanks to Plath and my interviewer and this job I don't want. And my mother. Feel the breeze, Girls, my mother says. Soak up the sun, she says, her gorgeous face tilted back.

***

I also tell my interviewer I'm from the Plains. Like Nebraska and Kansas, I say, but not Nebraska and Kansas. She looks puzzled. It's just that my part of the Midwest is not often known for being part of the Plains, I say. She looks puzzled again. "Where is Nebraska in relation to where you grew up?" she says. Now I know we're both lost. My interviewer changes the subject. Unless you are close to a river, I want to continue. Then the hills pick up. It's my reaction to her questions. "You lived here and then you lived here and then you lived here?" Yeah, sort of. Yeah, kind of. *Sure?* Okay, so I'm squirming. In my chair. Because it's been a long time since I was asked these sorts of questions. "How would you discipline?" she goes on. *Discipline? What discipline?* I think you isolate the problem, right? Re-direct. Try distraction. Don't yell. Go over to the kid. Bend down. Whisper in his ear. *Do that again and you're dead.*

***

Her hands on my abdomen, my healer says, "You've got someone buried in there." Oh, great, I think, now I'm the bad patient not progressing, in my garden not perennials but tombstones, half sunk, pitched at angles, like we're at sea. Or in a Scooby Doo episode. Nauseous, I consider my brothers. My brother from Mom's second marriage that recently ended in divorce. "Good place to end," my healer announces, the credits starting to roll, just as I'm about to crash into someone's birth date or death date or the word, *Beloved*.

***

Jacob, my half-brother, is born when I am 21. My mother is 45. At 8 he is an uncle. Don't let your babies touch my things, he tells me and my sister. For his party he says, No kids. He is gorgeous and smart and the three of us from Mom's first marriage take him under our wings. Welcome to the family, we say to him when he is fully grown. His friends find us fascinating when, living half-continents away, we randomly appear. "We've been over this," he tells them. His girlfriends sized up, his choices for college and work, we are dubbed, 'The Brother,' 'The Sisters,' and give him pep talks over the phone.

***

I call my sister. I'm a bad Mom, I say. "No you're not," she says. Oh, yeah, I say. I don't like the PTA. I mean, well, you know what I mean. "Yeah," she says, "I do." And I feel like if I don't keep everything perfect, it'll all come crashing down, I say. "It will," she says, "I've been in your house." And I don't cook anything from scratch, I say. "Everything is always different from the way it's supposed to be," she says.

***

Our youngest wants a Piñata for her birthday. A traditional piñata. On the contrary, the one she chooses, I decide, is otherworldly. Like a spaceship. Silver and light blue. Ready to take off. Like the mod balcony the contenders of the "reality" show, Top Chef, stand on to smoke their cigarettes. In Miami. They are up what seems like a million floors. Or the "shop" in the show, Miami Inc., where the tattoo "artists" whoosh in through a glass door, and the ocean (we can hear it) lands its waves near a concrete boardwalk whose gleaming and tanned fly on their glinting skates and bikes and "boards." Kind of Jetson. Kind of strange.

Miami. It's on my mind. And unlike Nepal and Liberia, it's not under siege--I can go there without *having* to write a will. Without my family panicking, my girls crying, my husband coordinating a back-up plan. Entailing congressmen and news conferences and military vehicles. And I won't need shots.

***

One of the last warm days, there are deer. Down the road. They look at me kind of expectant. Like they knew I was coming: Yep, there goes another one. Like that. Our youngest says, "But where do they *go, really*, in winter?" Yeah, where do they *go?* I think, *with her*, kind of mad and defiant, *I chime in. Show me* a tangle of trees woven tightly enough to keep the elements out. *Show me something* that I can show my kids.

***

A clerk at one of our local book stores asks me if I'd be interested in coming to one of their late-night book club wine things and I try to explain why it wouldn't work for me: I'm a writer (a real writer). I write at night (and sleep during the day). The clerk sniffs. "That's nice," she says. "How fun." What she means is, "No, you're not. I've never seen you on Oprah. And where is your book? It's certainly not here." Okay, so she's right. I've never been on Oprah and my work hasn't been stocked in their store. It'd seem paltry next to the huge glossies with their poster-size glamorous shots of the authors they choose. Maybe I'd fit in if I marketed my work with free stuff. Have giveaways with my poems. I could offer a bottle of St. John's Wort with each copy. A full spectrum light bulb. A can of Jolt.

***

Our oldest leaves us a message. Like Hansel's and Gretel's. A trail of adhesive-backed plastic jewels. They're on her Ipod, her notebooks, her phone. I lie awake thinking, This is what you do with song. This is what you do with code.

***

I hold the phone up to the washer. "See," I say to my sister. Sounds bad, she affirms. You can come over here and do laundry, she says. "Sure, I'll break *your* washer," I say. "Then we can go to the Laundromat together. Drive all over town looking for quarters. Get buzzed on candy from the vending machine. Watch *The Munsters* on the Laundromat's TV." My sister thinks this is hysterical. "Sure, because your washer is never broken," I say. But you wash *everything*, my sister says.

***

I say to my sister while looking at one of my lists, "Do you ever notice how people outside our family correct us about our past? Do you do that to people?" I say. No, she says, never. And I add that to my list: Do Not Correct People About Their Pasts.

***

I call my sister. I'm starting a new phase. Here's my new book project: How I turned retro, shabby chic, vintage, and spa in a matter of hours. In part one I'll explain how I quit trying to mask our unremodled 70s kitchen and went full throttle. Played up Brady Bunch orange. In part two I'll describe how I pulled the curtains and bedspread from our room and let the dogs drag them around the yard. In parts three and four, I'll detail how I raided your closet when you weren't home, took notes in your oldest's immaculate room. "No fair!" shouts my sister. Look, I say, I don't know anyone else who still has clothes from high school, and your oldest can teach us a lot about tranquility. Your secrets or mine? I say. "Okay," she says, stepping in between me and the stupid bully. "Mine."

***

Mom calls from San Diego and reels off headlines: San Diego, It's The Place You Learned to Walk, she says. There's a Breeze Like No Other, Surfers Galore, Indescribable Scents and Smells, and One Heavenly View. Another Place I Have To Go, I think. But not now. I need more time.

***

I tell my dad to come home. And when he doesn't, I turn on every fan in the house. So maybe we'll take off. And go where he goes. Ride above the city. Look out of the windows. Laughing. "Look, there's your school! Ha! Ha! It's so small! It's not where I thought it was!" I'll say to the girls. Because it's always a surprise. Being in the air.

***

"I'm a goldfish," I say to my husband. Every three seconds is new. So once I pull out of the drive, I'm on my own. With little memory of how I got there before. Except for maybe some sound and light. A vibration or two. The girls have been directing me from their car seats since they could talk. Turn left there, Mom, remember? one of them would offer in her high-pitched voice, having pulled her passie out, stowed her juice. "Yeah, I remember," I'd say, cheerfully, happily, accepting the help. "Thanks, Beautiful," I'd say. "Thanks. Okay, we're almost there. We're almost there." Uh-huh, the other would say, wrapping her blanket securely around her thumb. Hold my foot, she'd say, and I'd reach around while still driving, face forward, and hold her the best I could. While we made our way. Home.

***

I tell the girls it's a family curse. That *my* orthodontist was mean. Mostly, I remember his big thumb descending toward my mouth just after he'd twisted together wires tight enough to kill me. And, no, I didn't wear my headgear. And, yes, I promptly stopped wearing my retainer moments after leaving his office for the last time. But I was fifteen. And Mom was too busy, years after the divorce, trying to feed us, to notice. "So you're cursed," I repeat, to the girls, who are listening, thoughtful. "You're stuck. Bad Karma," I throw in. "I didn't follow the rules." What exactly is Karma? they ask, not buying into my attempt to lighten the situation. "What goes around, comes around," I say, running my tongue over my somewhat straight teeth. Feeling to my core in its entirety how this logic fails.

***

I tell my sister that I got lost after I left her house, that it strikes me as odd that the Culinary Institute of America promotes itself as the CIA. Don't they have a lot of bizarre happenings on a daily basis? Rogue spies showing up? Annoying clicking in the background when they're on the phone? Letters with blacked-out names? What a clerical nightmare, I say. I track down, through interlibrary loan, *The Littlest Witch*, my favorite book as a young child. It puts me in a kind of state. A Fall state. A Halloween state. A festive state. A hopeful state. Looking at the illustrations. Where being cold all the time is not at the forefront. But on a back burner on low. In a cauldron. On simmer. I buy cinnamon scented pine cones. I buy a cinnamon scented candle. I go back to being lost on the myriad of side streets leading to and from my sister's house. I emerge on a main road. I bee-line it home. I light my candle. Put my pine cones in a bowl. Wash the dog bowls. Fill them to the top. Scrub the bathtubs. Wash the shower curtains. Put socks on. Crawl in bed. And dream. I sleep deep enough to dream. Say to no one in particular I'm putting things on hold.

***

I drive over the edge of two curbs in my usual distracted state. Whoops. A few days later, my husband notices a large scrape on the back bumper. Maybe it was one of the curbs you drove over, our youngest says. "Would a curb do that?" I say. Probably not, my husband says. But he knows. Side mirrors have a short life on our cars. And I've probably driven over every curb in town. I'm usually driving slow. He just flipped you off, Mom, one of our daughters will notoriously offer as a car roars past. Flipping off. They know what it means because of my driving. It brings out the best in people. I'm in the way. Unless I'm on a mission. A kid is sick. A dog is bleeding. We're late for school. Otherwise, I'm in the way of commuters who just want to be home. Now. Yesterday. "So," I say, "it was probably me." Nah, my husband says. Later, I'm examining the damage under a harvest moon. Trying to remember the hit.

***

Our youngest hands me a website. http://www.boardingschoolreview.com/equestrian. She says she's been thinking a lot about things. That there's a way out of her current situation. Horses are the answer. We can visit, she says. I sigh heavily. I'm almost out of steam. "You'll miss us," I say, handing the piece of paper back.

***

Some guy calls about our cable, asking me if we want to upgrade. Look, I sigh, I don't even know what we have.

***

Call Mom, says my sister, when I say hello. "Got it," I say. Then my cell or hers gives out. It was code anyway. On the way to my car in the dark, I imagine the feel of a handgun at my spine. I shiver and pick up speed. Call myself sicko. I'm in the Maryland countryside. At an out-of-the-way elementary school. Remember this, I say, grabbing a piece of paper. Are you alive? says my sister when she reaches me. She's breathing heavily, like she's running. She just may be running. I can't breathe, she says, my chest hurts. "Where are the girls," I say, "Your husband?" Home, she says. Have you seen the moon? "Yes," I say. More code. It's getting cold, she says. Now. Finally. "I know," I say, slowing down. I've almost reached my car. "I just got out of volunteer training," I say. Making small talk. "I couldn't hold still. The presenter was doing the best she could. I'm such a loser," I say. "Dead weight." Code again. My sister gets it. Too many years in school, she says, making more small talk. "Wow, the wind is whippy," I say. "And all this rain. Light steady rain." Then we're cut off again. But back in our cars. Driving home.

***

I finally realize what Trunk or Treat means (I'd envisioned it as people standing around in a gymnasium with open treasure chests while costumed kids sashayed from trunk to trunk) when one of my best friends emails me she's had it and that she "sent" her husband and kid out to figure out what to do with their trunk and her husband came back with a back-end full of dirt complete with fake tombstones, a Grim Reaper costume for him, a skeleton costume for their daughter, and a nun costume for her. Aha, I say. I get it now. And I'm so impressed (as are the judges--they win first prize), I have this renewed surge of respect for Halloween. As a kid I cringed thinking about the upcoming "holiday." Not out of fear but the dread of feeling uncomfortable in a stupid costume and trekking from doorstep to doorstep, bowl to bowl, and falling in an exhausted sweaty heap with a blazing headache from having to look cross-eyed out of a plastic mask with poor ventilation. Enough, I say to my crabby self. And I try to make my inward self match my cheery outward self for the night. And I halfway succeed. It's a start. And my children (one who is blazing through a friend's neighborhood and one who has spent months looking for the perfect gypsy accessories) seem especially pleased. And I wonder if this is the key to life. Finding inspiration, even one dark eerie spot of it, and milking it, using it, to get on, making myself as happy as I purport myself to be to the world. Who cares if it's a bunch of tombstones and a trunk of dirt. My best friend all decked out as a nun. Leaning on the side of her car while her husband does all the work.

My best friend all kicked back, gazing down on everyone, her giant cross glinting at the little vampires rifling through their loot.

***

I tell myself to start with hope. I stop by my sister's but she's not there. I finish a book. I buy two gingerbread house kits for the girls. I drive, cutting back the night, cutting through the night. I go to the grocery store and stock up. I buy barrettes for the hair that always hangs in my face. I dust. I Windex. I recycle. I hold my breath, like the girls have taught me, while driving by the cemetery. I house hunt. I consider Christmas lights for the outside. I buy lettuce for the girls' guinea pigs. I do not surf the web to find out how much more successful my fellow writers are. I get out a cookbook and make a plan. I'm breathing you in, god, I say. I feel my father at the top of my head, in my brain. Waiting for me to let him go. Just above my eyes. Where all the tension is. I'm trying to finish this, I say. But I don't know how. And that is the truth. I just don't know how.

***

Supposedly shame is passed down from generation to generation. And like the music of a poem that people refer to, I don't get it. Poems don't "sound" to me. They take up residence in my chest. *Oh*, I'll cry out, my eyes brimming. Because of the good pain. I think it's like that with shame. You can use it. You can use, "You will never be what you should be," to go somewhere else. I think that's why my father wanted to leave. And take us overseas. Doing the only thing he knew how. Starting from scratch. Pretending another country was his until it really was. My father leaves a penny when I say this. I'm in the shower. It's clean. You got it, kid, he says. My eyes brimming. I turn the water hot. Hotter. Steam myself into the jungle of Africa whose edge we lived on. Steam myself down to the coast of Africa whose edge we lived on. I look across to the continent that we'd all, our family, eventually go back to. Full of its kind of trees. Like sand and ocean are pure to the recipient. Like air. Like steam. My love for my father is pure. My love for my father hurts. *Oh*, it hurts. But there is no shame. Never, ever shame.

***

I imagine my father standing outside my mother's sanitarium looking up. Peering at her window. Under stars. This is how I will imagine him for the rest of my life. He is giving his life to her, in the way that it will be. She is inside making the promise to give her life to us, him, in the way that it will be.   It is done.

He goes inside.

Five years later my first brother is born. Guitar-playing, art-making, country-traveling younger brother. In the waves of our father's first wake.

***

I call my sister to ask her what shape the diamond on Mom's wedding ring from Dad was. I can almost see it on her finger. Jutting up from white gold. While I'm looking at a diamond on the floor. My niece answers. She's meeting the Cross Country coach at the firehouse, she says. Giggles. He has an all-night shift. He needs to sign something. "Your mom," I say. My niece laughs. "Tell her to call me. She's not picking up her phone." Okay, says my niece giggling again. The firehouse is just up the hill; I imagine I track my sister down in one of the bays. She turns toward me just as she's handing the guy a pen. Breaks into a wide grin. You are nuts, she says. "I have to know," I say, the impostor, the fake solitaire, in my pocket, "What was the shape of Mom's diamond?" We walk out together. She doesn't remember. I can see Mom's hand. It's my sister's hand now. Mom's turning the faucet for the bath to the left. Hot. High. I'm a kid. I say something like, "Why do you never take it off?" It's so loose it slides to the left on her thin finger. So I won't lose it, she says. Steam filling the bright bathroom. Up past the pink tiles. It feels good. Warm.

***

In one last-ditch effort, I call Mom. What was the shape of the diamond on your ring? I ask, leaving a message. I'm on my dying cell phone. Sliding cents into the Salvation Army pot outside Walmart. It swings as if empty. My body hurting in the cold.

***

She doesn't call back.

***

Then she does. "It was circular," she says. (Like the one I've been toting around for days.) "Called a sapphire. I sold it. And you should have seen where it later appeared. I'll have to tell you about it sometime." Then the message ends.

***

He ordered the package, my sister says. She is referring to one of the teenage boys she supervised over the weekend. I go to the desk of the hotel to make sure everything's okay and there's a charge from this particular room. It was a package of PORN, my sister says. "Dear god," I say. "What did you do?" I called all the parents of the boys who stayed in that room, she says. It was the logical thing. I let them confront their boys and figure out who was responsible. One parent couldn't get off the phone fast enough. She knew it was her son. She knew the truth. "Dear god," I say. "Only you."

***

Our youngest says we need two suns. That if we had two suns we'd never have to go to sleep. We are driving by a stand of Christmas trees. A few all lit up. Suddenly the car is filled with the scent of cold, fresh evergreen.

***

I pretend the car I'm following is god. In a minivan. At home my husband is preparing our Christmas Eve meal. What have I gone out for? Ice? Sour cream? The usual suspects. More napkins. Carrot sticks. Dip. I drag the bags inside. Where it's steamy. And the girls are spun up. And the dogs are perplexed. And my husband has the usual look on his face. Kind of haggard. Kind of befuddled. Kind. I march around and try to bring the dogs and girls to order. It's impossible. And my gut is killing me. It's Christmas Eve and we're the religion-less. And I'm all about stalking god.

***

Preter. I don't get. I look it up. There are too many possibilities for each word. Past, by, beyond, more than. Preternatural. Supernatural? Past natural? Beyond natural? More than natural? "She is preternaturally mature"? She is "outside the bounds" of being mature? Preterhuman? More than? I was once mature, human, but now I'm not? I held it in my grasp, I let it go? A whole other world?

***

That according to the National Highway Traffic Safety Administration in 1971 one human life was worth $200,725. That this calculates, for one family, my family, in 1971, a brother, two sisters, a mom, a dad, to equal $1,003,625. Plus the family dog. An Irish setter. Sam.

***

I disappear into details. I tape up our oldest's room to paint. I jack open the fans. Clean their blades. I dust the insides of drawers. I use the shredder like it's going out of style. I sharpen all the pencils. I test the markers. I vacuum stairs. I throw away single socks and earrings. I wash the washer. I sneak old stuffed animals to the trash. I line up gift cards with minuscule balances. Clean out my purse. Throw it away.

***

My healer says it's time to head to the Labyrinth. I hadn't told her about my plans to go. I say, "okay," and about fall off the chair. She says, Do you know how to do it? I say, "no." She says, You sit on the benches on the periphery. You decide on your question. You walk until you get to the center. You wait for your answer. It'll hit you over the head, she says. The problem is figuring out what to ask.

***

It's not that my father's file never comes. After "Tab A" the CIA places my father's teenage work history. The family farm. A pizza place. "Tab B" separates his protest of something I don't understand. "Tab C" is followed by an explanation. That he was present for bad things? And wept once. It was brief. As if I had run away.

***

I'm at an amusement park. The girls, my husband are on a giant water ride. I'm standing on wet pavement watching people run by. In seconds a wall of water rolls toward me. I'm watching it. I'm standing. I'm sopping wet.

***

I'm in some kind of terminal. I'm little. In front of every few chairs is a monitor. It's 30, 35 years ago. The monitors look like small, older TV's. The chairs are plastic, fixed. The outer wall windows. All I see is sky. "*This* is a memory," I say to myself. Then, "The technology doesn't match the time. It's too current." Then, "I don't quite know where we're going." My sister and I dance around. Mom fiddles. The screens are dark. We're about to find my father. Go backwards. Through glass.

***

In Miami there are trees, water, a beach.

In San Diego there are old relatives. A famous architect's abandoned building that I've always wanted to see.

***

From a crack in the sidewalk, I sweep out a penny. Barely recognizable. Our youngest cleans it off. 1968, she says. Don't you remember? I found it the other day. "Okay," I say, leaving it, getting the protocol. "What is 1968?" You were four, she says, riding away. I pick up a handful of blooms knocked off by rain. Our oldest leans out while holding onto the door.

***

I'm driving above the city when I come to terms with the word, Blizzard. I slow almost to a stop before the guy coming toward me will pass. And then I'm climbing into another blast. Memory doesn't serve me. This is new. I want to be seen. But the pain is insurmountable. What is true may have happened and may have not. But the hurt and love coexist. And forgiveness. Out of all of it, I just want to be known.

***

And then there is a long silence. I pull the car into a hollow and wait. Our oldest daughter dropped off. The radio low. Earlier there were hands. Over and over, I have to look down, startle. Remember there is a road. That it is my duty to find the road.

***

I swing so low I can't write my way out of it. Then it is summer. On the wall where we vacation is a plaster plaque like the kind you'd make in grade school. While still wet, the artist had sunk in shells. And signed her first name. Mine. She dated it 1973. Later I pick up a penny. 83. Yeah, yeah, I say, to the heavens. Which in this case is a gargantuan rectangle of sky slung over a sparkly sea. Framed at times by our balcony. Who cares that the place is a dive. We brought sheets. We sleep and are soothed by waves. That ebb and flow. That make me weep. Then the sea birds catching drafts. Our youngest feeds them, annoying other beachcombers. Bite me, I think, throwing potato chips at the sky. An old guy walks by draped in a faded version of one our towels. Later, another gorgeous geezer, the spitting image of my blue-eyed father, strolls to a counter where I seek out ice water, cokes. I paint my nails pink. I eat *breakfast.* For days I'm struck dumb by the idea that people *drink* milk. I learn to text. I marvel at my life. I don't marvel at my life. I accept my life. I try to break out of my life. I realize upon reading a sign about who has the "right way" that it means the person having the "right away" gets to go "right away" as in immediately, first, and that my not having the "right way" never meant I was wrong. It just meant I was there. I decide the only class worth teaching is where the student begins with what she knows. Moves to what inspires her. Then dreams. I decide the only evaluation worth giving is response, coupled with the disclaimer, This is just my personal, subjective, piecemealy, fatigued but heartfelt response. Take it or leave it. Then I ache all over. And I ache all over again. And my healer says, Enough. We can't, we won't go back to what hurts you anymore.

And I consider, briefly, that she is drunk. Because, of course, pain is gain. Then I snap out of it. And I listen to her. And I go on.

About the Author

Katherine McCord was born in Monrovia, Liberia, Africa. She has an MA in English/Creative Writing/Poetry and an MFA in Poetry. Her first two books are *Island* and *Living Room* (prose poems). She has been published widely in literary reviews and journals, such as *American Poetry Review, Margie, Caketrain* and *Paragraph*. She has been a recipient of numerous awards, including, in 2011, a Maryland Individual Artist Award.

www.ingramcontent.com/pod-product-compliance
Lightning Source LLC
LaVergne TN
LVHW040116080426
835507LV00039B/382

9 780982 922842